GIFT OR CRO

Charles Gillen

Gift or Cross to Bear
By Charles Gillen

ISBN - 978-1-906657-48-2

Spinetinglers Publishing
22 Vestry Road
Co. Down
BT23 6HJ
UK

This book has been formatted by
Spinetinglers Publishing

FOREWORD

What you are about to read is not meant to scare or frighten you, that would make what I have written quite pointless. I am relating to you experiences which have happened throughout my life from childhood to my adult life, which take place in a lot of people's everyday lives, maybe more extreme in my own personal life.

I hope by reading this book that you can get some answers to questions that you were always afraid to ask. I would like to think that it would ask you to question yourself not as a person, but a human being, with all that being a human being is, with all our insecurities, doubts and, frailties and except them but more so to accept your mortal soul which is eternal, strong and never dies which is the most precious Gift from God that we should cherish.

GIFT OR CROSS TO BEAR

I believe there is a lot of evil in this world and it takes all shapes and forms. Some are so cunning and well hidden, that we tend to accept this as normal; but this evil tries to consume us on a daily basis when we are too busy to notice, when we are trying to get on with our everyday lives. There is still a lot of good in this world if we only took time to notice. We have forgotten all the simple things in life like prayer: prayer is speaking to God, speaking to Jesus Christ, prayer is one of the most powerful things we can do as human beings but we have to believe or start believing again or praying again. Jesus will welcome you back at any time with open arms. You may have had a crisis in your life where you may have thought God has abandoned you and you blame God for what has happened. If you let this seed grow you will have eventually abandoned God and your faith and evil has won. Most crises that happen in this world are manmade; although difficult to get through, understand and cope with at the time, this is the time we most need God. We all have a Guardian angel who is appointed as the keeper of our soul when we are born, who will stay with us all our lives even on our death bed so that we will not die alone, who will then carry our soul to heaven. Do we acknowledge or speak to our guardian angel enough? They give us guidance through everyday life. Every day if we would only open our ears and listen to their advice, God has an unending army of good angels that we can call upon at any time for help, through prayer whenever we need them, this is the power of Faith and all we have to do is pray and truly believe.

Through personal experience, I know what it's like to lose my faith, although at the time I hadn't realised that I had lost my faith. My first child was stillborn 8 months and 2 weeks into the pregnancy. My wife gave birth normally, both of us waiting for our first child to be delivered, knowing the child would be stillborn but both of us hoping and praying that the doctors were wrong, maybe they made a mistake, praying right up to the point when our baby girl was delivered, only to be a stillborn. My wife said it was, "*like waiting for a present only to open it to have nothing inside*". My reaction at the time was to blame God for everything. I stopped praying, I stopped believing in God at that very moment. If I only knew then the impact of the words that I had dared to say to God Almighty would have on my life, I would retract them humbly and beg on my knees for his forgiveness. This is the moment that changed my life forever. I blasphemed, and shouting at the top of my voice, "*What kind of God would do this to me and my wife*". I said I did not believe in God, I was so angry with God. We only had two weeks left until our child, a little girl Donna, would have been born. Looking back now twenty four years later I have a fresh pair of eyes. Still births happens all the time and there are numerous reasons why they occur. I should have handled it differently. I now have an angel in heaven who had not to endure the trials and tribulations of this life and she is always by my side every day even more when I need her. It took 20 years for me with the forgiveness and trials that Jesus Christ offered me as a Gift, to redeem my soul which I have accepted in Jesus Christ's name.

DEMONS

We have all heard stories of demons, devils, ghosts, do they exist in our modern world or are they restricted to ghost stories of a bygone age or modern day movies, do the dead walk the earth, does purgatory exist, is there a heaven is there a hell? We all have experiences which sometimes cannot be explained and because we cannot explain it we just shrug it off as if it had never happened, not giving it a second thought. Some people are more perceptive to their surroundings than others and souls and demons can pick up on this and try to use you as a means to their advantage.

Do you ever get a shiver as if someone has just brushed past you, have you thought you have seen someone out the corner of your eye, you look around quickly and no one is there, do you even think twice about it. This happens to numerous people every day its souls looking to see if you can see them, and if you can see them or feel their presence normally you have a Gift which you can accept or decline. The souls are trapped here in purgatory maybe until the end of time and you are a messenger chosen by God as an intermediate to help pass them on to heaven. Souls are constantly looking for that person, if you accept this Gift you have to go through a series of trials were you will endure things not of this world to hell and back. How you accept this Gift or even know you have it is left in your hands, there are no set rules and really no one can help you, search as you may, you are on your own. But remember whatever happens to you, that you are doing God's work, you will be frightened, you will see creatures not of this world, who are among us daily in our everyday ordinary world. The only difference now is that you can see them and feel their presence and they know of you and will do their best day and night to stop you doing God's work. They are now very real to you and will manifest themselves daily and some never leave. It can become very surreal; you will eventually tell people of what is happening to you. Some people are open minded and will believe you, others will dismiss you as crazy and some will not want to listen to you because you frighten them. Your own faith will be tested to its limit. A good night's sleep will be a distant memory. You are at your most vulnerable when you are on your own and at the early stages you will do anything not to be on your own. But there will be a lot of times you will. If you live alone it could drive you to madness, thinking that you are going insane. When the trials begin they are very frightening and very hard to endure. The trials are to identify how strong your faith is in God and if a Gift from God is for you. At any time you can decline the Gift, it is not for the weak. You have to be strong willed and strong in mind and strong in your faith. If the souls know you are a messenger, so does Satan and all his wiles of hell will persecute you constantly attacking when you're awake more so when you sleep and more so when you are alone, when you are at your most vulnerable. The trials will continue until your faith in Jesus Christ becomes so strong you will become a soldier of Christ, only then will you wear the full body armour of Jesus Christ, a helmet of salvation, a breast plate of Righteousness and your Sword of Faith and if you are a Messenger of God you have to be a pure soul so then Satan wants your soul even more. Once you have the full body armour you are totally protected from all evil. This is when your faith is unshakeable. There is a lot to endure to reach this point. Now the fight to save souls in Jesus Christ name begins as it has been from the beginning of time and will continue until the end of time. As a messenger of God you are truly blessed and should be eternally grateful for this Gift. As a child growing up in the Troubles in Northern Ireland where there is war, there is evil. Evil is what creates hatred shootings, killings, bombings all senseless killings young people barely left school with guns in their hands, filled with hatred and this is where evil thrives.

TOUCHING EVIL

As a child I couldn't sleep with the bedroom light off because of souls and demons, as I know now, but I didn't know then. In my room I could only see images on the wall and transparent faces of devils under the bed but I couldn't tell anyone as who would believe me? Bedtime was always a living nightmare for me, knowing what was waiting in my room for me, I did not know why this was happening, I attended Sunday Mass and confessions every week. I would go into the chapel on my way home from school, I was as a good boy, and I would pray for my family every night. The demons would instil fear on me daily. I could not go upstairs in my house on my own. Praying to God to take them away and make it stop. Each morning I woke I would leap down the stairs in huge jumps as each morning something was around my shoulders and clinging to my back it used to terrify me, this continued for years throughout my childhood. This scenario has a happy ending as I found out in later years that a small boy lived in the house before me and had lived in my room, he wore leg callipers and had to be carried down stairs on someone's back every morning and had died at an early age, his soul was still here in now my room he needed help to get downstairs each morning of his young life as he could not walk without his callipers. His parents must have carried him on their back each morning. His soul was still here, he had not left for some reason. Sometimes souls do not know that they are dead. I was a child myself and I did not know what I was experiencing, all I could feel was someone on my back every morning. He needed help to be passed on, which at the time I was unaware of. These are early experiences I can remember which I had no control over that just made me very scared. All these experiences seemed to stop one day as I entered my teenage years, although the memories never left me and then started again with a vengeance almost thirty years later. As a child I was born into a Roman Catholic family, in a Catholic society. I attended Mass every Sunday and went to confessions once a week. On Holy days our schools would take us to Mass. Catholic religion was taught in our schools. Religion was a big part of my life. I would pray every night before going to bed. I had a great fear of dying when I was a child and always wondered what death would be like; imagining what heaven and what hell was like. I used to ask myself the question why? Why life and why death. What was it all for and then I would scare myself as I had no answers. As a child I was always asking questions and looking for proof even of Gods existence.

BEGINNING OF MY TRIALS

I was working away from home, staying in bed and breakfasts with work colleagues and at this particular time I was in Templeogue, just outside Dublin. It was September when I first arrived at the bed and breakfast we were shown to our rooms, the room was quite large with two large single beds and an easy chair in one of the corners, it was a very respectable area Templeogue although each driveway had security posts to keep cars from being stolen and it had endless rows of trees in each culde-sac and all the gardens were kept very tidy.

Breakfast for us was 6:45am then off to work returning around 6pm each day Monday to Thursday, on Fridays we finished 12:30 then I drove back home me to Derry. I stayed in this bed and breakfast quite a lot, sometimes six weeks at a time, which I dreaded because of what was waiting there for me each time that I returned. At this stage I had acquired a small bible a gift from my sister which I couldn't be without.

It all started one evening, I had just returned from work, got changed and showered I was sitting on my bed alone on my computer when I could feel something in the room, I hadn't experienced this feeling so strong before. The feeling took me back to my childhood, it had been that long, fear ran through my whole body every hair follicle on my body was standing on end, as the presence got closer to me the more my heart rate increased and the more terrified I got. At one stage I felt paralysed as it seemed to consume my whole body, I couldn't move, I tried to shout out but words would not come. I started to say the Lord's Prayer in my head, *Our father who art in heaven hallowed be thy name*, I seemed to be praying forever, its grip tightening on me, it felt like it would never let me go. I kept reciting the Lord's Prayer again and again. Finally it released me, the room was as cold as ice. I opened the bedroom door and ran downstairs as fast as I could to the dining room, the house was empty I was on my own, I had decided I was not going back into that room, not that night anyway. I sat in an armchair facing a settee, on the settee there was another presence, just watching me. It just sat there; it was shrouded in a black dust like veil. I decided to try and ignore it and not to look in its direction. I got up to make a cup of tea, when I felt it behind me, following me, the more I acknowledged it, which was hard to ignore, the stronger the presence got. I could feel it putting pressure on my lower back. This was a different presence, a different feeling from the presence earlier in the bedroom, it was more threatening and it seemed to thrive on my fear and the more I acknowledged its being, the stronger and more powerful it got. All I could do was begin to pray again and again. It did not like the sound of prayer especially the *Our Father*, on hearing the prayer, it disappeared through the adjoining wall into the next room, and it had left for now. I had received my first gift from god, my sword of faith, words of prayer from the bible. These words from the Lord's Prayer seemed to inflict so much pain on this demon that it could not bear. I had been given my first weapon against evil, which I always had, but did not know how to use it. We all are given the word of God in various ways, even something as simple as prayer, if we truly believe the words that we are saying when it comes to confronting evil face to face it is the most powerful weapon that we can possess. The more people pray the less evil there would be in the world today. We all need to have faith and increase and strengthen our faith on a daily basis.

One of my colleagues returned later that night I explained to him what had happened to me earlier that day, I had to tell someone, and I wanted to change rooms. He would have been in his late fifties and very open minded and a good friend he had been through a lot in his life and was the salt of the earth. I needed to talk to someone about what had happened that day and he just was there. He said some people can sense and see what others can't and that I would be ok; never the less we swapped bedrooms that night. That night in my colleague's room I was awakened by what looked like three souls at the bottom of my bed. They just kept looking at me very intriguingly, but kept their distance. I pulled the blankets over my head and went to sleep. On return to Templeogue the following week it was just me, my colleague had been sent to another town, the key was normally left under a plant pot at the front door. On arrival the house was usually empty although there were other people staying in the bed and breakfast, they were all out at work. My heart sunk as I lifted the key with room number 2 on the key ring, I was back in the same room. At home that weekend I had mentioned to my wife some of what had happened, I did not want to frighten her, she told me not to go back to the house, but this was my work, I really had no choice.

I placed the key in the door and turned it, as I stepped in I was met with a presence in the hallway which followed me upstairs running past me to room 2. I opened the door, placed down what bags I was carrying and started to unpack for the week organising my shirts and trousers, hanging them up in the wardrobe. As I was doing this the presence sat in the easy chair in the corner watching me, each time I looked in its direction it would look back at me and its presence would start to get stronger, so I decided to try and ignore that it was there, this seemed to work. I took my bible out of my suitcase and placed it on the bedside locker, this did not seem to bother the presence, I said the Lord's Prayer, the presence never moved. It was then that I realised that this presence was a soul. There was a local community centre which I used to attend to give me something to do at night, it had a gym which I used most nights after work and after unpacking I went there. On my return from the gym I entered the house and as most nights the house was empty, I was met with the presence in the hallway, it followed me around the house as I was preparing my meal, this presence was not threatening, it seemed more anxious, as if it had something to tell me. After my meal I went up to my room followed by the presence, it wasn't bothering me as much this time.

Later that night I was watching television when from the side of my eye I could partially see the presence, which I now knew was a soul in the bed next to me. As I looked towards the bed I could see at first a girls leg slightly bent up at an angle and she was lying on the bed as soon as she knew I could see her, she sat up slowly at first and then she leapt off the bed and spoke to me, "*Can you see me, you can see me, you can help me*". This frightened me, I didn't know how to respond is this good or evil, I still was not sure, I had to get out of the bedroom again and made my way downstairs to the living room, were I stayed until later that night until other residents came in, then I went to bed. Later that night around 3am the presence was whispering to me as I was sleeping, "*I was murdered here; you can help me, you have to help me, let me show you what happened to me*". I answered no, again and again, no, I was scared, how could I help? She finally stopped asking me, that night any way. When I awoke the next morning she was still there. The next night when I was going to bed, she was there again. When I started to sleep, again she kept asking, "*Let me show you what happened to me*". She kept repeating this over and over. I woke up and for some reason that I didn't understand at the time I said, "*OK show me what happened to you"*. *S*he immediately took possession of my body for the next few minutes which seemed like a lifetime. It felt as if I was her in her body, I was looking through her eyes, I could feel her fear, she was very frightened, I was experiencing everything that she had went through, everything was very real as if it was just happening now. The bedroom was now a hospital room I was dressed in a blue hospital gown sitting on a hospital bed, there were tubes coming from my body. I remember a tube coming from my inner thigh which was restricting my movement also tubes coming from my arms. The nurses were dressed in old uniforms, their hats had two sides which met in the middle, grey hats with a red badge in the centre, they looked like uniforms during the First World War. The nurses were speaking to me, I could feel fear and anxiety as the nurses approached me. One had a large needle and the other nurse took hold of my arm with the tube hanging from it, holding it very firmly, the other nurse with the needle proceeded to insert the needle into the tube in my arm as I struggled to get free from them I felt very weak and couldn't get away, the nurse said, "*Now the more you struggle the harder this will be for you*", at that she pushed and squeezed the syringe into the tube in my arm at that moment my eyes closed, they had killed her.

I slept the rest of that night until the morning. Next morning at breakfast I asked the landlady had anyone died in the bedroom I was staying in, "*No*", she said, "*and I have been here the past 35 years and no one has died in that room*". She seemed very annoyed that I should ask her such a question. After finishing work that day I decided to go into some archives for the Templeogue area were the bed and breakfast was situated, to my amazement 1862 the

Templeogue Lunatic Asylum was once situated were the bed and breakfast was now built. Why was this girl from over a hundred years showing and telling me this and asking for my help?

My sister had a lady, who said she was a medium, around to her house one evening, and had gathered a number of friends. During the meeting she quite impressed my sister and her friends, she said something which regarded me, although she had never met me and my sister had told her nothing about me. She said that I had a Gift given from God and that I should contact her if I wish and she told my sister to give her telephone number to me. My sister contacted me and told me what she said, I decided to phone the lady, maybe she could give me some answers, when I rang and spoke to the lady she told me her name, I told her who I was and some of the experiences I had gone through. She told me that I had a gift which I could accept or decline I needed time to think, she said she could see a huge white aurora around me, but a part of it was broken, I asked her what she meant, "*Your faith,*" she said, "*you have lost it along your way in life, it's up to you to get it back.*" I told her I had started praying again and carry my bible everywhere I go since the experiences started again, she told me, "*If the souls in purgatory know you can see and help them evil also know you have a Gift and will seek you and your soul.*" I told her I would accept the Gift from God, she then told me that someone was there with a message for me, a very small woman with black, curly hair who was very determined to talk to me saying she knew me very well. She had described my Granny Hannah, I asked what she wanted and the 'medium' told me, "*She says what you're doing, accepting the Gift, is right but you will have frightening trials ahead, I will be with you through them do not be afraid."* Anne asked me to pray with her, after praying I asked Anne what do I do to help souls, she said you can help pass souls from this world by praying with them and giving them guidance, I asked how and she answered, all in Jesus Christs name, there will be some souls you will not be able to pass on, Jesus Christ will come for them. I was still unsure and she said, *"Give it time, you will know what to say when the time comes, but you must strengthen your own faith in Jesus Christ."*

On my next visit to Templeogue a lot changed for the worst for me this was the start of my trials and only the beginning. It was now November, the dark mornings and short dark days. The demons now knew of me and my Gift, at this stage my faith was still not strong enough, I prayed every day, even in my sleep I would pray to make me a strong soldier of Christ. As well as demons each day I could feel the presence of my Guardian Angel and all of God's good angels. This is the most amazing feeling of love and protection which is really indescribable and what's more amazing is that anyone can experience this love and protection if you believe in Jesus Christ it's that simple. When I entered my usual room the soul of the girl was still there, I told her I would try and help her. Her presence got stronger, I was frightened. I asked her to pray with me to God, we said the Lord's Prayer. Although we prayed, she did not leave, she stayed. Each time that I returned to the bed and breakfast she was still there, maybe my faith at this stage was not strong enough to help her.

FIRST EXPERIENCE

I was in my bedroom in the bed and breakfast and had my first close up experience with evil. A black ball like cluster of dust particles came at lightning speed through my bedroom window and stopped directly in front of me, then forming until it stood up, so close to me, by the mercy of God all I could see was its black shape and formation, I could not see its face, which I was thankful for. I froze, what was this thing standing in front of me? The temperature in the room dropped, it was freezing cold, all I could think of was to pray, I started to say the Our Father. As I spoke these words it was as if they were weapons that seemed to inflict pain on the demon which it could not bear. The demon shot through the wall into the adjoining room, it was gone, but only for a short time, it was not long before it came back again. It now was lurking around the room and each time that I prayed it would leave for a moment. I knew at this stage that I had to increase my faith. Was Jesus Christ showing me what else was out there? Why me? With all that he was showing me any thoughts of disbelief of God existing, the questions of is there a heaven is there a hell were disappearing rapidly. How could I not believe? Just believing was not enough. I felt guilty, all those people in this world with blind faith who accept God and the bible without question, I was a doubting Thomas from the day my angel a stillborn was taken from me to heaven, I felt like she had been stolen from me and I needed someone to blame. I decided what kind of God would let this happen and that I didn't want God in my life. Jesus was now, after all this time, giving me a chance to redeem my soul and help other lost souls as well. How could I not accept? I needed to have the faith back that I once had as a child and I could feel it growing each day.

Each trial, although terrifying at the time, brought me nearer to Jesus Christ and all his good angels and my guardian angel who never leaves me. If only we could all see them, it would be so easy for us all to believe. I have been blessed and I am eternally grateful for a second chance, which is offered to all of us on a daily basis all we have to do is open our ears and eyes and accept God's love. Prayer is one of the most powerful gifts we have against evil, all evils, which exists and runs rife in this world and in our everyday lives from domestic violence to murderers, paedophiles and wars all over the world. There are whispering demons who put evil thoughts in our head, and your guardian angel telling you what's the right thing to do. Do you ever start to pray and forget the words? This is demons at their work who don't want you to pray, when this happens start your prayer again and again until the words begin to flow.

Going to bed one night I had read my bible and said my prayers, I now began to leave a light on as I slept, like I did in my childhood, as I could feel the fear beginning again. It was not long before I began to drift off to sleep when I felt a presence at the bottom of my bed, it was evil, the demon was back trying to possess me and take my soul. I felt it starting with my feet, with great pressure, numbing my body as it crept upwards, inch by inch, closer to my face. My first test of my faith had begun, I struggled to move, my mouth closed shut I could not utter a word, it was my faith, my prayers, my belief in Jesus Christ that was my only defence, my weapons. I called to Jesus Christ to protect me, I prayed the Lord's prayer time after time believing every single word that I was saying, I was gradually gathering my body armour, my breast plate of righteous, my helmet of salvation, my sword of faith.

After what seemed like hours the demon released me. My faith had saved me that evening, but this continued every night afterward and my faith was continually tested. Going to bed was something which I now dreaded. One night I heard voices in my room, it was a group of angels who were there to keep the demon away from me, I had been praying for one good night's sleep as I awoke each morning at 6:30am for work usually physically and mentally exhausted from the night before. The demon was at my bedside the angels stood around my bed forming a circle, I heard them speak to the demon, *"Leave him alone, let him sleep."*

It was the best night's sleep I had in a long time. The demon now increased to demons, and pursued me during the day as well, always staying in the background, waiting until I was on my own before showing their strength. It felt like a group of them jumping on me trying to gain entry to my body. One day in class I had a room of twenty students, there were demons at the back of the class, they looked like small child-like creatures and seemed transparent and they could move at very fast speeds. I observed the class, it was very quiet as they were completing an exam, the room was silent and the pupils unaware of what was happening. As I looked around I could see some of the pupils had white auroras around their bodies, a bright white light, some brighter than others and some had none, no light at all. As I watched, a demon walked up alongside one of the pupils with no aurora and just stepped into the person's body. I was shocked at what I had just witnessed. Was this person possessed and did they even know? Should I say something, would they believe me? I decide not to say anything, the thought which crossed my mind watching the demon stepping into the person's body was that the person seemed totally unaware, this was a frightening thought.

All of us can have demons without knowing, to rid ourselves of demons we have to ask Jesus Christ to Purge our bodies and souls everyday through prayer and by the way we live our lives and by taking a good look at the way we live our lives. We need to be prepared to change, you don't have to be a murderer to go to hell, just a bad person. There are millions of souls in purgatory walking this earth who don't know why they're there and don't know how to leave.

CARLOW

Working in Carlow I was staying in a rented three bedroom house which was shared with my work colleagues, on some occasions I stayed there on my own. It was on these occasions the demons would persecute me, mostly taunting me at first. When I first arrived in Carlow as I opened the door I could sense that there was a presence in the house, I can always feel first if something is there. As I brought my suitcase and baggage into the house the presence seemed to be everywhere throughout the house. I went to the bedroom to unpack and then went downstairs to the kitchen to cook something to eat for myself. As I was cooking the presence in the house began to walk close by me time and time again. I decided that I would try to ignore it, as I did not know what it was, it was very persistent and kept on walking by me, making its presence stronger each time, the goose bumps began to appear on my arms, I turned to look at it, I could not help myself. It now knew that I could see it. It was not a lost soul it was a demon sent from hell and it was not alone the house seemed to be filled with them. I was on my own in the house which made it worse for me. I went to bed that night and as I got into my old habit of leaving hall lights and bedroom lights on I went to sleep.

I had only been sleeping a few hours when around 2:30am I was woken on hearing voices in my bedroom, to find my bed was surrounded by demons, taunting me, very childlike taunts like, *"Can't sleep with the lights off,"* and, *"Call yourself a physic, you can't even make us go away."* They were laughing at me. At this stage my faith was still not strong, it was terrifying, some of them were on my bed, I had my bible beside my bed, which I reached for and held it as I began praying. It was the summer and daybreak was around 4pm. As the light came through the bedroom window they left. They returned each night and I couldn't make them stop. My life was like a constant nightmare and I felt lost, I asked God how this could be a gift, sometimes I thought that I was losing my sanity, or I was imaging all this. Then I realised that I was being shown evil and thought how lucky I was. I thought to myself, if every person in this world could experience five minutes of evil, to show them that demons exist, would it change the way they think of God. What consequences would it have on their daily lives and their attitude to some peoples questions, is there a heaven, is there a hell. All their questions would be answered.

Each night as the demons returned to torment and persecute me, even with their presence, I   prayed constantly for Jesus Christ to strengthen my faith, but really that was up to me. If you're not a very strong minded and strong willed person, and have no faith in God, I really do not know what the outcome would be if you were put in this position. At the beginning the demon would be directly on top of me in a matter of seconds. It was like a physical fight to get free of the demon; this was made more difficult as sometimes your body felt paralysed. My only defence and main defence was prayer, and believing every word in that prayer, as if every word spoken was like a spear or sword striking at the demon until it could not take anymore, until it finally released me.

Other experiences at the beginning can be just as horrific when the demon would stand at the bottom of my bed and, starting at my feet, would creep up my body until it was fully on top of me. This feeling is very terrifying at the beginning, as it crept up my body trying to consume my soul my only defence was my faith, these where trials. I prayed to God, saying each word of my prayers as slowly and clearly as I could and for the first time in my life understanding what the words meant and how powerful that prayer is, "*Deliver us from evil*", how many times had I recited the Our Father and not understood the true impact of what I was saying. I was fighting this demon through prayer, it tried to paralyse my body, I felt my body numbing, the more I prayed the stronger my faith got and the stronger my body got. This made my fight with the demon harder, but I was now the strong one and the demon finally gave up, for then at least. This fight continued every night for two years and still continues every day in my life. I started to pray in my sleep and still do. I can sense a demon entering my room when I sleep and by prayer can keep it at bay. Demons are sent by the devil, it wants our souls and will never give up until the end of time. We have to protect ourselves from all evil. How do we do this? Do we need weapons? How can we defend ourselves from things we can't see? It's very simple, believe in Jesus Christ with all your heart and soul, ask for his forgiveness and pray. Prayer is the most powerful gift we have from God and is the strongest weapon we have, the Bible is the word of God, Our Sword of Faith. We can all ask God for a full body armour against evil which is a helmet of salvation, a breast plate of Righteousness and a sword of Faith. When you can feel this suit of armour on your body, you are protected from all evil and truly blessed, all we have to do is believe in God. If we truly believe we are truly protected and all evil dissipates to dust. A lot of my experiences happen to a lot of people in this world who shrug them off as bad dreams or nightmares, who would believe you? Maybe if more people would talk about and share their experiences there would not be as much evil in this world. The devil and his demons play on our human nature and all our weaknesses. Too many people would not like to be ridiculed, made fun of, and told that they're insane because of experiences that they can't explain.

DUBLIN PRIEST FATHER KAVANAGH

In the early stages of accepting my Gift, every day and more so at night I was tormented by demons, everywhere that I went they would be there. There is something about the darkness that they seem to thrive on. During the day they would seem to hide from the light. But any darkened room or any unlit room they would show their presence fiercely and even more so if I was on my own. This took its toll on me at the beginning. They wouldn't let me sleep at night. During the day after work in the bed and breakfast they would watch me and follow me from room to room and at night would try to possess me. I knew I couldn't go on much longer like this. I needed someone to talk to, maybe a priest. I found a priest nearby in Tallaght where I was staying. That weekend I went home and decide to telephone the parochial house in Tallaght. I spoke with a priest, Father Kavanagh, briefly explaining my situation. He was very understanding and said I should come and have a chat with him, we arranged a time for the following week. When I left the bed and breakfast at 7:15pm that night, there was more than myself in the car, the car was full of demons, angrily attacking me. But I was protected, as if I had a shield around me, while they seemed to be so close to me, so close that the hairs on my neck stood on end, they couldn't reach me. But that did not stop them trying. I recall that it was a particularly cold winter's night as I pulled up outside the parochial house. As I stepped out of the car and proceeded to the front door. I could feel all of the demons on my back, trying to tear at me. I rang the doorbell and Father Kavanagh opened the door. I introduced myself and he welcomed me in. The demons could not enter. This was a house of God, my sanctuary. In the hallway of the parochial house there was a huge life size picture of Jesus Christ, he looked so natural, almost like an ordinary man, it was a very humbling picture. It made me think what Jesus Christ went through for us as a human being. We sat down and began to talk. Father Kavanagh listened very intently and was very understanding, as he spoke there was a presence standing behind him at his right shoulder. I told him what I could see and this at first seemed to frighten him. He asked me if it was good or evil. I told him it was someone who he knew who was watching over him, that his hand was on his shoulder. He was relieved. We spent a few hours together but he couldn't give me any answers, but that our talk had renewed his faith. He admitted to me that he would pray in the parochial house most nights by himself rather than go to the chapel, but from tonight on he would be going to the chapel each night to pray. He said I had a gift from God that he could not explain, during his time as a priest he had never experienced any souls or any evil and that he would pray for me and asked if I could pray for him. As I was leaving he gave me some bracelets with Our Lady Mary on them, which I thanked him for. The demons were waiting for me as I made my way back to my car. This was the only time that I had spoken with father Kavanagh and I never met him again, he could not help me.

MALLOW

In the course of my work I travelled a lot, mainly around southern Ireland and on one occasion I found myself in Mallow. On arrival at the bed and breakfast I parked up outside, the house was old, a detached bungalow, it had a garden and some flower beds. I was met at the door by an old gentleman, who invited me in and offered me tea or coffee, to which I accepted. He went to the kitchen and returned with a pot of tea and hot scones with jam and fresh cream, this was not the usual welcome at most bed and breakfasts. We chatted for a while and then he showed me to my room, which was on the ground floor, the B&B had at least four bedrooms. I followed him down along a very dimly lit corridor, and my bedroom was the last bedroom on the left, looking out to a side garden, the window had net curtains. The room was compact, with an ensuite, very high ceilings, a glass panel above the door and one bedroom window. He left me to settle in and told me I could use the dining room to watch television. I unpacked and settled in for the night. The wardrobes and the bedroom furniture were mahogany, very old worldly. There was a big double bed. This was the month of August and the temperatures were around twenty degrees. This was to be the worst night of my life. As I had to get up at 6:00am the following morning I started to get ready to settle in for the night. It would have been around 8:00pm. The room began to get ice cold, so cold that I had to put on a fleece and tracksuit bottoms and a woollen hat, clothing I used for the gym. My teeth began to chatter. I stepped out into the hallway and the temperature was very warm. As I stepped back into the room I could feel the ice cold temperature only within the bedroom. As I closed the door I looked around the room I could see outlines of what I can only describe as creatures, all different shapes and sizes. They were coming in through my closed bedroom window one after one and then taken up different positions in my bedroom, until it was filled to capacity. There seemed to be no end to them. As I looked at the bedroom door I could see this really tall figure, which looked like a man. His head was above the door, were the glass panel was, which was almost seven foot high. I was getting very frightened at this stage and could feel myself beginning to panic, I did not know what to do. I lifted my phone from the bedside locker and dialled Anne's number, there was no answer. I tried several times. I was getting colder and colder and these creatures kept coming in. Anne finally answered the phone. I could hardly speak by this stage I was that cold. I told Anne what was happening, my teeth chattering together as I tried to speak. She said maybe someone in the house was messing about with an Ouija board and what I was seeing was old spirits as well as demons. She told me to be strong, that they couldn't hurt me, to pray to Jesus Christ to protect me. I was on my own. I crept into bed still fully clothed, I sat upright, in the bed. I was too scared to lie down. I reached for my bible and started to pray, as I prayed and stopped to look around the room not believing what I was seeing. If I focused or stared at the small child like outlines of some of these creatures, they would charge straight towards me. I soon realised as the night went on if I outreached my hands and said, "*In Jesus Christs name keep your distance from me.*" It would stop them from getting close to me, but they kept charging at me all night long until I was exhausted. Something huge, almost the full size of the bed lay down beside me, I could not see this creature, just its huge bulging outline and could feel its coldness. The whole room felt like death. This creature's presence was terrifying, but all it did was lie there. Every time I would move, I would brush against its coldness. It was if it was waiting for its moment to consume me. By now it was 3am I was exhausted and fell asleep, but only for a few minutes. They would not let me sleep. I was awakened by something pulling me by the arm until I was almost half way out of my bed and it spoke to me, *"Who said we couldn't hurt you?"* They were referring to the phone call that I had made earlier. I replied, *"Do you call that hurting me, is that the best you can do?"* I knew that I had to be I strong and show no fear. I was awake again but too tired to sit up straight. My heart rate had increased, my heart pumping in my chest it felt like I was doing a cardio session in the gym. Were they trying to give me a heart attack? I then realised God works in mysterious ways. For the past six months I had added cardio into my daily training sessions, was Jesus preparing me physically as well as spiritually for this night, my worst trial. As I lay down trying to ignore what was going on around me, which was almost impossible, I began reading my bible, which didn't seem to be working. I had to believe in God with all my heart and soul to get me through this night. If I can get through this night with Jesus Christ by my side, I felt I could get through anything. I prayed and prayed as they kept attacking me. As I looked up to the ceiling, the light was turned on, I dare not turn the lights off. I could see what looked like a mist swirling around the light shade. It then began to take shape and it was joined by an endless parade of these creatures. The creature then formed, it had face like features, but no solid body and it looked like smoke or a mist, just hovering above me in the air. When I looked at it the creature looked directly at me, it then came towards me at speed, stopped directly on top of me and put its face on top of mine so close to me trying to enter my body. It was so cold and seemed lifeless, its mouth on my mouth as if was trying to drain my body of life, it felt so cold, its breath was ice cold. Praying as hard as I could, it seemed like it was never going to leave, they never said a word and as each one left me, there was another one and another one to take its place, they were relentless and endless. I jumped up, they stopped but the other demons and other spirits in the room took their place constantly attacking me. I prayed for Jesus Christ to come and make all this evil go away. I had never been as scared in my life and realised if I shouted for help and someone did come, would they be able to see them, or just think that I had lost my mind. I did not know what to do. I realised once I acknowledged that I could see them that they would attack and try to frighten me. I couldn't lie down, I couldn't sit up. I looked at my watch it was 5:30am, my time to get up, it was daylight outside. I got out of bed and got changed into my work clothes. They started to leave my room. I had made it through the night and suddenly realised that Jesus Christ was with me all through the night or I wouldn't have survived. I went off to work that day feeling very tired, it had been a long night. Although it lasted nine hours it seemed like an eternity. A night I did not want to through ever again. On return to the bed and breakfast that night I stopped at the chapel, my only place were demons couldn't follow me I stayed there for about an hour, I could have stayed all night. I made a point of finding the nearest chapel to where I was staying, which I visited every day; it was the only place that I felt safe. When I opened my bedroom door and entered, the spirits and demons began to enter the room, not again, could I go through another night like the previous. I left my room, went out to the car and went for a drive, I was not alone. Some of them followed me to the car I was truly terrified, was this going to continue every night? I pleaded with Jesus Christ in tears. What did he want me to do, what did I do to deserve this, I felt a sense of hopelessness, I could see no end to what was happening to me, I felt lost. This was my lowest point. Who could I turn to for some help, for some answers? Shouting as I was driving to God above, if anyone saw me they would have thought I was mad. I drove back to the chapel. The only place I felt safe.

The chapel was quiet with only one or two people. I walked around the chapel stopping to pray at each station of the cross. There was a life sized statue of the crucifixion of Christ at the main door on the right hand side. It was white marble and so life like, I had to reach out and touch it. I stayed there until the chapel closed. I prayed and as I prayed I had this overwhelming sense of comfort and peace and protection, as if someone had put their arms around my whole body and had lifted me out of this world, it seemed to last forever. Everything that had happened to me, all my experiences began to make sense. This experience made me cry very sorely, I couldn't stop. This was my first experience of the love of Jesus Christ, which he has for us all. I felt truly blessed.

I returned to my room, I went through another night with the spirits, demons and what I can only describe as creatures. But this time with more confidence and a much stronger faith, I felt more ready for what the night would bring. I had Jesus Christ on my side. Romans 9 verse 31 *"What shall we say to these things? If God be for us who can be against us?"* Romans 9 verse 38 *"For I am persuaded, that neither death, nor life, nor angels, nor principalities, nor powers nor things present, nor things to come"* Romans 9 verse 38 *"Nor height, nor depth, nor any other creature, shall be able to separate us from the love of God, which is in Jesus Christ our lord."* Reading my bible that night, all through the night, the readings from Romans read very true for my situation. They kept me awake all night; although this night did not seem to be as bad as the previous night. I had one more night to stay in the bed and breakfast but I knew I could not face another. I was tired I had not slept in the last two days; I phoned in sick to work and went home. I have never had an experience as bad or severe as that since that day. It was like being shown what else was out there in this world and what hell would be like. Although I would not wish my experience on anyone, I feel truly blessed that Jesus

Christ has given me this experience and opportunity.

Charlie Gillen

SOULS IN PURGATORY

When people die and leave this world their body is what dies. Not their soul. Depending on how a person has lived their life and their actions, and choices that they made determine where they go next. A pure soul will go directly to heaven; a bad soul may go to hell. Then there are the majority of souls who are in purgatory for their sins, where they do penance. Some will be there for a short time, others for hundreds of years, some until the end of time. What can reduce the amount of time spent in purgatory is forgiveness from people they have hurt and prayers from them. Each prayer offered up takes them a step closer to heaven. Each prayer is a small step out of purgatory and a step closer to heaven. Our prayers, in my experience, can bring a soul from the gates of hell and into the arms of God in heaven. I meet souls wandering this earth every minute of every day, there are so many lost and have no idea what to do, and when I meet and speak to them it's usually their time to leave purgatory. When I explain how I can help them leave, they all say the same thing, "*Is it that easy.*" Most are in disbelief. When it's their time it is very easy. All the souls I have met look for me because they know I can help them. I have met a woman trapped in purgatory who was carrying what looked like a small child wrapped in blankets, but there was no child, the blanket was empty. Her child had died in infancy and she had blamed herself for the child's death and had been searching for the child since she had died herself, her guilt and grief and blaming herself for the child's death had kept her here for so long. As she left purgatory to go to the bright light of Jesus Christ's welcoming arms, her child was there to welcome her too. A lot of the souls are looking for loved ones or they have had committed sins in their lives and think that they can never be forgiven. I was painting an upstairs bedroom one afternoon when I felt someone watching me, He was sitting on the window ledge and he didn't speak, I asked him who he was and could I help him, he didn't answer. It was later on that night and getting dark when I had finished that he first spoke. He told me that he was watching me paint all day, and that I had done a good job, and that he wanted to let me finish. He then went on and told me what had happened to him. He was a Scotchman, who was in full Scottish dress; he was in a band and was marching, on this particular day his young son of about four or five years old was with him. His instrument in the band was a huge drum, which he hit on each side. His son was walking alongside him, as they were marching over a small bridge his son fell into the water and drowned. He blamed himself for his son's death and had been searching for him all these years, the man's story was very emotional and he made me cry. He told me not to waste tears on him. We talked and we prayed. It took a lot of talking to him, trying to convince him that what happened was an accident. When he left purgatory into the bright blinding light of Jesus Christ his son was also there to greet him. All the souls I have helped to pass on are reunited with their loved ones who have been patiently waiting for them. I have had other experiences not as nice. I went to bed early one night around eight thirty. I hadn't been sleeping long when I felt myself being lifted out of bed horizontally. I told whoever this was that this was not funny, were they trying to scare me and if they were it was not working. They put me down again.

He was dressed like a roman soldier, a centurion. He said he was trying to get my attention by lifting me out of bed, I said there was other ways to get someone's attention. I asked him did he need help.

He said yes but not for himself, but someone who had descended from him, a young man who I had met recently, who was in my home. He asked if Archangel Michael could protect him the way he protects you. He told me his name and I said I would do my best to help him. I had met the young man one night in my kitchen. My son had a few friends around for drinks. He was around twenty one. He approached me and while he was looking at a bible which was placed in my kitchen. He asked, "*Do you believe everything that's written in the bible.*" I replied, "*Do you read the bible?*" He told me he did so I said, "*Revelations 22 Verse 19. And if any man shall take away from the word of this book of this prophecy, God shall take away his part out of the book of life, and out of the holy city, and from the things which are written in this book."*

I showed him the verse, but he continued to be argumentative and had his own explanations. I told him that people can sometimes take their own interpretation from the bible. We talked a lot that night and as we talked it unfolded that this young man had a gift. Which he could not control, his faith was not strong, and he seemed to be losing his faith even more. Demons would appear to him on a daily basis. He could see them very clearly. They terrified him and told them he could not make them leave. I told him only his faith and his faith in Jesus Christ could make them go away. That he himself would have to pray to God for help. I offered to help him the best that I could. At this stage of my life I was only at the beginning of my trials. As the night went on he asked me a lot of questions regarding the bible

and asked me about my beliefs. He asked me to go
out to the backyard at one stage, I agreed, he was a
smoker. What happened next was something that I
had not expected. But it was quite frightening. As we
talked, I could feel a lot of activity behind me, it was
demons, they were everywhere and he could see
them. He looked terrified; he started crying, "*They're
all over your body, jumping on top of you.*" He put his
hands up to defend himself, sobbing quite hard by
this stage. I took hold of his both wrists. I said, "*They
can't hurt you.*" He said, "Yes they can." So I told him
I could make them go away and so could he with
prayer. I asked him to pray with me and to ask Jesus
Christ for his help, ask in Jesus Christ's name to send
them back to hell and to send us all his good angels.
He prayed with me. He said they're leaving, they're
leaving. He couldn't believe what was happening;
the demons never left him before, only of their own

accord. I told him he should pray to Archangel Michael he was the one who sent Satan to hell, and that he is always there for me. He said that I was the one who made them go away and that he could not do that. He then closed his eyes and it looked like he went into a trance. He looked straight at me. But not with his eyes, there was something inside him looking directly at me through his eyes. He placed both his hands on my shoulders and said, in a gravelly voice, almost a whisper. "*I am Lucifer; you don't know what you're dealing with.*" At that he pushed me so powerfully that I was thrown at least two metres into the garden behind. I immediately leapt forward, taking hold of his arms. He looked like he had just woken up. He asked me what had happened, and told me he couldn't remember. I told him he was possessed. We agreed to meet up the next night to have a chat. The next night he came to my home and we sat in the kitchen. He said that last night was good for him and if I could help him more that it would be great. He asked me a lot of questions about the bible, as he seemed really unsure. I brought my bible out and we searched through it for answers for him. As the night went on a lot of souls came into my kitchen. The young man could see them clearly, a lot more clearly than I could; he spoke to each of them in turn. Each one of the souls asked for my help and did not ask for his, as if they knew his situation and that he couldn't help them. They seemed to be avoiding him. As the night went on demons came into the room. When they appeared, the terror that appeared in the young man's face was only to be described as fear, desperation and a look of hopelessness. Each time they appeared, I could feel their presence and knew exactly where they were before they formed, but he could see them vividly and he knew he could not make them leave. I prayed to Jesus Christ, The Lord's Prayer. The demons disappeared through walls on hearing the Lord's Prayer, the most powerful prayer we can say. I asked the young man what he could see; he said a ball of black dust at first, then teeth and a face before forming completely. I never have seen a person so scared and so helpless to their own situation. We talked about the demons, he said they were in his house everyday taunting him, they said he could do nothing about it; he couldn't make them go away. I told him that he could, just as I had, through Jesus Christ, what he needed to do was increase his faith and believe truly in Jesus Christ, only he could do this himself, he had been given a gift, he had to choose how he was going to use it. I told him that the Devil knew of his gift and that he would pursue him daily to obtain his soul.

We are each given choices on this earth so we must be careful how we choose.

Other souls came in that night; there was a court jester from medieval times, who did not want to leave yet, which I thought strange. One lady came in and was reading my bible and said she hadn't read that verse from the bible in a long time, when asked if I could help her pass on, she replied no thank you, she went on to explain that she had only recently died and that she was staying to console her husband and her family that in their grief they needed her, she would go when they did not need her anymore. After that night I tried contacting the young man several times, he told me to keep away. I hoped he made the right choice.

*

A man came to me one night, he was very hesitant on asking for my help, and he said he had done terrible things that he was at the gates of hell and if I could help him. I was shocked by what he had said but I told him all I could do was pray with him and pray for him. That what he had done was between him and God. We prayed the Lord's Prayer and he said an act of contrition. The bright light of Jesus Christ shone down from the heavens. He went towards the light, paused and looked back to thank me for my help. All of the souls I have helped have come back at some time to thank me or have thanked me as they leave to go to the bright light of Jesus Christ. I been told by Archangel Michael that I am a messenger for souls in purgatory, here to help them when it's their time, to help and show them what to do. All of the souls I have met are lost, wandering aimless in this world, some do not know that they are dead. They still stay in their once own homes, among the living. Some souls I have met are being kept here unknowingly by their loved ones, who through grief cannot let them go. One young girl I met had only recently died; she was seventeen, she told me that she felt she had to stay to be with her parents, who had cried every day since she had died. She said to me, if only they knew and could see where I am, and how happy I am, they wouldn't be so sad. I told her it was her time to go, that grief for some people takes a long time to get over. Some people never get over the loss of a loved one. I asked her did she want to leave, that it was her time. She said yes. We said the Our Father; she went to the bright light of Jesus Christ and was gone.

Other souls I have met are in what I can only describe as dark places, trapped in places where there is no hope as they see it, they appear to be curled up in a ball without movement, hidden from any light which they seem to repel. When meeting these souls, it takes a lot of coaxing to get them to come forward, even to talk to them. Most of them believe that whatever sins they have committed are unforgiveable from their point of view, they have given up, and they think that they are beyond any salvation. When I meet these souls, it's their time. When I explain this to them, that they can leave this dark place and go to Jesus Christ and let God decide, a lot do come forward, we pray and they leave, some souls have been in their dark places for a few hundred years, their purgatory.

Charlie Gillen

OLD SPIRITS

I have encountered old spirits only a few times. Some of them trapped in their own surroundings, waiting for someone to set them free. When you first see them, it can look like a faded image of a face, the more you look at it, the clearer the image becomes. When this happens they know you can help them enter this world, because you can see them, and they know you can see them. Each time this has happened to me, I have asked Archangel Michael for guidance. He has always told me to try and ignore them and not to look for them. I have seen some of these spirits in the bark of trees and the more you watch the face forming the more evil it looks, they seem to feed off someone knowing that they are there. I have never looked long enough for them to fully form. It is as if there is a gate which can be opened and they thrive of the energy of someone who can see them.

LOST SOULS

There are some souls which cannot be helped, for various reasons which are unknown. These souls will be in purgatory until the end of time, when Jesus Christ himself will come for them.

SUICIDE

I believe when a person commits suicide that they have exhausted every avenue and can see no other way to solve their problems in their everyday life, although they leave a lot of unanswered questions to relatives and friends left behind. A lot of us think of suicide as an easy way out, even a coward's way out, but to the person contemplating suicide it is usually well thought out, and well planned. Whatever personal views we hold on suicide we cannot truly understand what makes a person end their own life, it's between the person and God, who are we to judge? This brings me to a soul I met on a motorway on my way to work in Belfast one morning at around 6am. As I was approaching near the end of the motorway going into Belfast I could feel and sense a soul who was a woman, she seemed to be running in all directions in the motorway not knowing where she was going or what to do she seemed very disoriented and was looking for someone to help her. I thought that she did not know that she was dead, although I could feel that she was happy and relieved, but also seemed very confused. At this point on the opposite side of the motorway as I looked across I could see a bus and one police car, in front of the bus there was a dead body covered with a white sheet, it was the soul that I had met. She was now coming in and out of my car going back to the scene were her body was, she was still very confused. I began to talk to her; I told her that she was dead and that she would be alright and that she had to make her peace with God, I asked her if she wanted to say the act of contrition and she said yes. I then told her that it was her time to leave this world and that I could help her, I told her to say the Lord's prayer with me and that Jesus Christ would come for her, that she would see a bright light that she should go towards. We prayed and Jesus Christ sent his white bright life and she left this world. Later that day on the news it said that a woman had walked on to the Belfast A6 motorway directly out in front of an oncoming bus.

Charlie Gillen

EARLY STAGES

At the early stages of my gift, I was terrified to do a lot of things, which I would have done on a daily basis. If it was dark I wouldn't go out to the back garden on my own, even if it was just to put rubbish in the bin, because as soon as I stepped outside my house, it seemed like an army of demons were waiting for me, trying to instil as much fear into me as they possibly could. I used to ask my wife to accompany me, and she did, as I told her what was happening to me since the beginning, she must have thought that I was losing my mind, and believe me so did I. No one else could feel or see or experience what I was going through every minute of every day, more so and more intense when I was alone. I had received a gift of a bible from my sister. When I eventually told the rest of my family what was happening to me. My family had all sorts of suggestions; some said go see a priest, others said that I could refuse the gift and that would make it stop. I went first to see a local priest, as I stepped into my car I was accompanied by demons in the back of my car, who just seemed to be laughing at me, they knew that I was grasping at straws for answers and who would believe me? When I reached the parochial house, I was met at the door by the priest, he welcomed me in. This was the first time that I noticed the demons couldn't follow me, my refuge. We sat down in a small room in the parochial house. This was the first priest that I was going to tell of all that was happening to me, I felt that this was going to make things better, make everything alright. We spoke for almost an hour, I was doing most of the talking, the priest mostly just listened, I got the impression when he did speak that he didn't believe me, although he didn't actually say that. What he did say was that he had never experienced anything that I had told him. I asked him if he would come and bless my house, as there was a demon that never left my bedroom and he agreed to a night and a time, Thursday at 8:30pm. As we were saying goodnight he said something to me which I have never forgotten. He said that he knew a real holy priest a lot more holy than him that I should talk to, and that I could call anytime to the parochial house. The next night I called back to the parochial house at the same time, the priest answered the door quite vexed and surprised to see me back and told me that he was going out and that I should have made an appointment. This was not the person to help me. He did bless my house, but the demon stayed. I now began to realise that this was my fight and my problem and that it was up to me to understand what was happening to me. When I travelled to work some mornings, I left home at 2:30am to get there for 8.30am to start work, sometimes as far as Cork, a six hour drive. My drive was usually on my own, but the car was not empty, all through the night until day break, the demons would torment me, making their presence felt, I used to drive with the interior light switched on, to take away the darkness. My only defence was prayer, I would pray the whole length of my journey for Jesus Christ to make them go away, and it was so terrifying. The night was so long, daybreak, only a few hours away seemed like it would never come. When daybreak came it was like Jesus Christs light had filled the world and made the darkness and the evil disappear. These journeys for me were weekly, and I started to carry my bible everywhere with me. I would place the Bible opened face up on my passenger seat, I would pray for my Guardian Angel and Arch Angel Michael to protect me and for Jesus Christ to send all his good angels to protect me.

When I put my hand on the open Bible, I could feel good angels around me and I would ask them to pray with me. My journeys were getting more bearable, the demons hadn't left, but the angels had arrived, they were always there with me, all I had to do was reach out for them and acknowledge them. My faith was getting stronger, but my trials had only begun. I would speak to my guardian angel now on a daily basis and she would let me know that she was there and listening to me. To feel the presence of a heavenly angel is so amazing and so indescribable it's hard to put into words, it's like being held, comforted, protected, loved, you never want the embrace to stop. When this embrace ends it can make you feel light headed and sometimes a little disoriented. We all have a guardian angel that is with us from birth, which never leaves us, giving us guidance each day throughout our lives, if we would only listen to them, their guidance on even everyday trivial things, as well as the more important decisions throughout our lives, helping and guiding us. They are that little voice we hear in our head telling us what is right and what is wrong, what we should choose to do and what we should not do. Angels work tirelessly to protect us and our immortal souls, but it is our choice what way we live our lives, God has given us freewill to live our lives the way we choose. But he has also given each and every one of us a Guardian angel of our very own who is dedicated to protecting us and our souls. The prayer to Our Guardian Angel, which I was taught as a child just seemed like a rhyme as a child now rings so true.

"Ever this day be at my side to light and guard to rule and guide."

Such simple words but so powerful, if we truly believe what we ask for in this prayer. A lot of us never acknowledge our guardian angel as we go through our everyday life, because most of us cannot see them or feel their presence we tend to think they do not exist, like the prayer they are a memory from our childhood. We could not be further from the truth. Guardian angels play an enormous part in this world, trying their hardest to make people of this world choose the right path and to make the right and proper decisions, they have a tireless and thankless job, which they are dedicated to. The amount of wars, famine, killing, that happens in this world every day is of mankind's doing, our choice not Gods, we make our own choices. The world would be a better place if we acknowledged and listened to our Guardian Angel.

PROTECTION

We are sometimes sent relatives who have passed on from this world to heaven to protect us as well as our guardian angel. I was at a family gathering and began to speak to one of my sister in laws who I didn't see too often. She had two young children, one of her children was a little girl who was just over two years old, and as we talked she told me that her child had trouble sleeping at night. They had put her to bed in her own room and had a sound monitor placed in her room. Each night the child awakened screaming, her mother said that there was a lot of interference and strange noises coming from the monitor, when they went to her room the child was out of her bed and crouching in the corner of her bedroom with her hands over her eyes and screaming at the top of her voice. This continued for some time so they decided to contact a priest. The priest arrived and they told him what had happened, he proceeded to bless every room in the house, starting downstairs as the family followed him from room to room. When the priest came to the bottom of the stairs the young girl began screaming and would not go upstairs, her mother kept her at the bottom of the stairs and the priest proceeded upstairs to bless the bedrooms. He blessed all the bedrooms and told the parents that everything now should be ok and if anything else happened to contact him again. Since that night they had decided to move house as they still did not feel comfortable in the house, she said the room was always ice cold day or night. Although they had moved house her mother was still very worried about her little girl and asked me if there was anything that I could do for her. I said that I would do my best. Even though the little girl was my niece we lived in different towns and I only saw her at family gatherings and she would be strange if she did not know you. I told her mother that I would try to get close to her, so that I could feel what was around her. I prayed to Jesus Christ to give me an answer to put her mother at ease. As the child walked past me I stretched out my hand which just brushed past her, without actually touching her head. I could feel a strong presence, It was an elderly woman with white hair, she was crouched almost on her knees, with her arms around the child following her every movement. She spoke to me, *"This child is fully protected there is no need to worry*". I relayed this on to the mother as it was happening, I told her although she has her guardian angel watching over her, this is a woman who knows her, I was getting a name Kath. Before I could say her name the mother said Kathleen. Kathleen was the child's great Grandmother who had passed away some years ago and now she was looking after and protecting her great grandchild. The nicest thing then happened, the small child, my niece, ran towards me, jumped up on my knee and kissed my cheek. It was very emotional, her mother was so pleased knowing her child was safe and could not believe what her child had just done, jumping up on my knee. The rest of the day the child kept coming over to me. Her mother said unless her daughter really knew someone she would never approach anyone. This was the first time that I had used my gift for a person who was alive, up to this stage in my life it had all been souls that I had been helping.

EARLY STAGES

At the early stages of receiving the Gift I was visited a lot by some of my relatives who had died. Some would ask me to pray for them, others would ask me to pray for their own families, who needed our prayers as they were in a dark place. When this happened I would pray for them and get my family to pray for them. Each time that they revisited they would thank me for the prayers. This is when I began to realise how powerful prayer can be. Other times visits from my dead relatives were to give me support. In the midst of everything that I was going through they were with me and told me not to be afraid and that they were proud of me. This gave me great comfort and sometimes brought me to tears. Being given this Gift from God at the beginning was very daunting and very frightening and still is today. When I first told my family of the experiences that were happening on a daily basis, they immediately believed me, there was no doubt in their mind that maybe I was making it up, they knew what kind of person I was and that a subject as serious as this was not to be taken lightly. My brother's reaction was, how could I live a normal life with all the demons and dead people around me every day, it seemed impossible to him. One of my sisters said I should refuse the Gift, tell God I did not want it. My other sister said was up to me to decide what was best. My mother just accepted it. My great uncle who was eighty two years old told me not to get mixed up in any of it and to walk away. With all this advice I knew that I had to make my own decision. I decided I would keep the Gift and do my best. It was very difficult at the start because all that I came into contact with was evil, they would pursue me everywhere I would go night and day. Some souls would come through but at the beginning I found it hard to tell the difference as I could not see them, only feel their presence. It did not take too long for me to tell the difference. The main reason for accepting the Gift was that it was offered to me and it was answering questions that I had been asking God all my life. All my questions about heaven and hell and whether they existed, all my *Why q*uestions I asked as a child and into my adult life were being answered. I am blessed and thankful for this Gift, how could I refuse? It was not easy at the beginning coming face to face with evil and I do not think it ever will get easier. But when you have Jesus Christ by your side and you can call on Gods good angels at any time and can have Archangel Michael by your side, you have an army against all evil.

ARCHANGEL MICHAEL

In the early stages of accepting the Gift I prayed for protection from all the evil that pursued me in my daily life. This was when Archangel Michael came into my life and I thank him daily for being with me. Whenever I need his help he is there to protect me. One of the first times that I called on him was because of a powerful demon which was always in my bedroom. It always made its presence strong, this was one of the first demons that I had encountered, which was sent to persecute me. Each time the demon appeared in my room I would pray or read from my bible. I quickly realised that they could not abide prayer and the word of God. But this was only enough for them to leave the room and it was not long before they were back again. This demon was part of my trials. It would laugh at me at the beginning when my faith was not strong. I had a priest come and bless my house to purge my house of all evil and the demon; he could not see or sense the demon. I took the priest to my bedroom and the demon was there and the priest could not tell that the demon was in the room. Archangel Michael sent Satan to hell and I prayed to him to send this demon who was persecuting me to hell were it belonged and he answered my prayers one night. The demon was in my bedroom, that's where it normally would be unless the house was empty. If I was at home on my own it would follow me around the house. On this particular night I was alone in my bedroom and the demon was there. This demon seemed to me that it was never going to leave and at this stage I felt that I had enough of this demon. I knew my faith was getting stronger, but knew that I needed help to send this demon back to hell and out of my life. It sounds strange to say but this demon was part of my everyday life, when I tried to sleep, when I awoke in the middle of the night to fight it off me and when I awoke in the morning it would be there either showing its presence strongly or lurking in the shadows of the corners of my room waiting for me to show weakness. Although it never gave up I could sense from its presence that the stronger my faith in Jesus Christ grew the weaker its presence became. I began to taunt the demon, telling it that it was wasting its time with me, that my faith grew stronger each day and what more could it do to me that it hadn't already done. I went through all that it tried to do to frighten me and that I had put my trust and my soul in Jesus Christ's hands, that there was nothing else it could do to me, that I was not frightened anymore. I prayed to Jesus Christ and asked him to send me Archangel Michael to send this demon back to hell and he did. Archangel Michael appeared, he was dressed in gold armour with his sword clasped in his hand, and he was a huge angel, so powerful. When he entered my room all I could do was pray and I asked him to send this demon back to hell. I felt so humbled in the presence of Archangel Michael. As I prayed I became very overwhelmed with what was happening. I remember thinking a fight between good and evil was taking place in my bedroom. It really seemed so inconceivable. It did not last too long, but seemed to go on forever. The demon was screaming and screeching in its blackness. It was screaming that it could do nothing here that the faith was too strong.

A hole opened from nowhere in my room, it looked like a gateway to hell, which Archangel Michael sent the demon screaming through, the demon had gone. Archangel Michael said to me, *"Whenever you need me I will be there for you"*.

PLAGUE OF DEMONS

I have met a lot of souls over a period of several years, since 2009 when all this began again. I have come to terms with the Gift and what I was given the Gift for, which was to help souls in purgatory. Although this was my main purpose because the souls knew that I could help them. The demons also knew that I had a gift and have been persecuting me every day for the past seven years. I had decided that I needed to lead a normal life; being woken up every night with an evil entity in your room at the bottom of your bed begins to take its toll on your everyday life. I never have a complete night's sleep and as I sleep I pray until I wake up, which is usually in the middle of the night to be confronted with an entity half way up my body or on my back. Over the past year I noticed that the demons around me had increased, more so when I was alone. They were getting more persistent and were pursuing me more and more each day. They were beginning to stop any souls coming forward to me for help, they were beginning to put a wall up between us, which the souls were too frightened to cross. This had not happened before. There seemed to be more demons like a plague around me. I decided that something was changing, the demons wanted me and were not going to give up easily. Every day they made their presence felt. Although I am a strong willed person, physically strong and have a strong unshakeable faith in God, I decided that maybe this was the end of my Gift as I couldn't help the souls anymore because of the entities around me. I prayed to Jesus Christ for guidance and prayed and put my trust in God. I received an answer. Every person is given free will to choose what they do on this earth. I chose to accept the gift and it was up to me to refuse the Gift. I was told that the demons were a plague and that my trials were over and that it was up to me to take the righteous road. I thanked Jesus Christ for the Gift which he had given me and that I wanted to now return it, I was told that thy will be done it would be swift and that no souls would look for me again and neither would the demons. All my relations came to me from heaven and said that I had done the right thing, that God never wanted me to suffer demons and that from this moment on that they could not visit me ever again from that day, but that they would always be there for me and that we would meet again someday. I am hoping that my life will return to normal again.

GIFT OR CROSS TO BEAR

Some people call these experiences a Gift from God, which I agree with, if God offers a person this Gift it is totally up to that person to accept, we all have free will from the day we are born until the day we die and we will all be judged accordingly. You can do a lot of good for souls lost in purgatory with no way of escaping unless they meet someone with the Gift of helping them to go to Jesus Christ in heaven and reuniting with their loved ones. The souls wandering this earth know if you possess the Gift, so there are souls constantly looking for you day and night to help them. This was the most rewarding part for me, although it takes a bit of time getting used to having souls around you every minute of every day. I never liked calling them ghosts or dead people they were souls, like you and me who were at one time inside a human body, our soul never dies, it is are human bodies that die and the way we live our life in our human body decides where we go after this life. I am truly grateful for the Gift that I was given as it opened my eyes, I have seen souls in purgatory and have experienced angels from heaven and demons and devils from hell. I have experienced Jesus Christs love and I know we have a loving, forgiving God who would do anything for us; all we have to do is have faith. The down side in having the Gift is that all that is evil know you have the Gift as well and they will persecute you day and night trying to stop you doing God's work and will try to get you on the side of evil. It is a lot for a person to endure and from personal experience it can only continue for a certain amount of time. But remember we can give it back at any time. I still meet souls every day and I know that I cannot help them anymore, it is not their fault that I can feel their presence and it is very hard for me not to talk to them and try to help them, they are in a purgatory that people blessed with a Gift can see, feel and experience. I know that I will experience souls until my dying day. But my trials are over the demons that have plagued me all my life have left, they are gone from me. Jesus Christ is my saviour all my life all I had to do was put my trust in his hands. How simple is that.

THE END

Gift or Cross to Bear

Lightning Source UK Ltd.
Milton Keynes UK
UKOW03f1401180117
292266UK00002B/4/P